LIVING BETWEEN MATERIAL AND SPIRITUAL WORLDS

LARRY CYRIL JENSEN
BRIDGER LEE JENSEN

LIVING BETWEEN MATERIAL AND SPIRITUAL WORLDS

Simple
Existential
Phenomenological
Hermeneutical Ways

LARRY CYRIL JENSEN
BRIDGER LEE JENSEN

ISBN: 978-1-963565-83-6 (Paperback)
ISBN: 978-1-963565-84-3 (eBook)

Library of Congress Control Number: 2025904346

Printed in the United States of America

Published by:

info@thequippyquill.com
(302) 295-2278

UNDERSTANDING SELF AND OTHERS

HARMONIZING

CHRISTIANITY

EXISTENTIAL PHILOSOPHY

AND

PHENOMENOLOGICAL PSYCHOLOGY

Thanks to Catalea Collins for the lead she took in making this book come to fruition. Catalea was a driving force in editing, designing, and consulting.

Thanks to the many professors and students who helped educate me so that I could write this book.

Thanks to the freedom of beliefs and expressions so wonderfully protected and provided in the U.S.A.

Thanks for the blessings, miracles, and inspirational guidance, which I too often lack awareness and appreciation.

Thanks

PREFACE

QUESTIONS TO MAKE YOUR LIFE BETTER

I write to share with you questions and choices that can make your life more meaningful and productive. So where do we start? Let's start by answering some very basic questions about this whole matter of living. And no one else can answer these questions for you. I have taught at five quality universities, published scores of journal articles, and written many psychology books but it is not for me to decide for you. You must answer the questions for yourself. I will try to give some helpful tips but eventually, you must be the answer-giver.

Now, you will find here a pattern or sequence. First are questions and later there are choices for you to make. The first question is about yourself. For example, "What am? Do I have a conscience? Am I free to choose my life? Am I free to live my life?"

The second set of questions is about truth and knowledge, and these are followed by a third set about your identity. These are basic questions that you addressed long ago. These are very deeply held beliefs and you probably will want to hold on to most of your old answers. That is just fine but at least be consciously aware of them to do a good job in making future choices for your life.

The choices will be presented in the second half of the book. The choices in the second half are related to the questions and deal with: what kind of being you will choose to be, how you will choose to understand others, and what kind of relationships will you choose to have.

These questions and choices may seem a little strange for you to be dealing with now. Most books would present them as information for you to comprehend, remember, and apply. Not here. The answers and choices are to be of your own making for it is your life. How you respond will determine the amount of genuine freedom, joy, and success you can experience during your life.

INTRODUCTION

USING YOUR EXPERIENCES TO MAKE CHOICES

There is no better way to learn about life than through personal experience. So let us use and lean on your personal experience to answer questions about your life. Let us also learn by choosing among alternatives for in almost all things there is opposition or at least an opposite; good and bad, strong and weak, ugly and beautiful, honest and dishonest, true and false. These never-ending differences can lead to oversimplifications, rigidity, and dogmatism if approached unintelligently. But they truly cannot be ignored for opposites constantly appear in life and just a study of any language will show that adjectives almost always have opposites and are essential in making sense of the world.

There are several ways we can interpret the opposites that we inevitably encounter. We can deny their existence but obviously, that will not lead to much wisdom. The second approach would be to choose between the opposites but qualify by considering where and when and in what context we make the choice. For example; is hot better than cold, is loud better than quiet, and tact better than honesty? Well, you say, "It just depends." And it certainly does depend on where, when, and with whom or what we are dealing with. Sometimes we must make a choice and act and at other times we can choose both opposites.

For example, in one of the choices you are asked the question; "Are people are free agents or are they determined by heredity and environment?" The difference or choice is between defined logical opposites, but it is true that sometimes a person could be a free agent and at other times, or in certain states, be almost completely determined by heredity and environment.

The value of answering questions and making choices among opposites is that it leads us to greater learning while learning from our personal experiences. There is no surer or dependable way to learn about self and others than examining and interpreting everyday experience. It is much better than being told what to believe for here you know the truth in a more genuine way and furthermore, it is more convincing than being told what to believe by another. Also, you can learn through making choices with your heart and feelings as well as with your intellect.

At this time, you may be skeptical about whether you are the best person to make these choices and answer these questions but give it a try. I will wager that you will find it both interesting, enjoyable, and more yielding of truth than being told what to believe.

TABLE OF CONTENTS

SIX SECTIONAL PREVIEWS...ix

SECTION I: "QUESTIONS ABOUT YOUR EXISTENCE"............................1

SECTION II: "QUESTIONS ABOUT YOU AND YOUR SPIRIT"............25

SECTION III: "QUESTIONS ABOUT YOUR IDENTITY"......................41

SECTION IV: "QUESTIONS TO ANSWER ABOUT TRUTH AND
KNOWLEDGE"..57

SECTION V: "CHOICES YOU CAN MAKE ABOUT YOUR BEING"......71

SECTION VI: "CHOICES ABOUT UNDERSTANDING OTHERS"..........85

SECTION VII: "CHOICES ABOUT YOUR RELATIONSHIP WITH
OTHERS"...97

ABOUT PROFESSOR LARRY CYRIL JENSEN....................................121

ABOUT BRIDGER LEE JENSEN...123

SIX SECTIONAL PREVIEWS

SECTION I: *"QUESTIONS ABOUT YOUR EXISTENCE"*

Is there another world?

Living in a world with more wonder.

Am I more than just brain activity?

Does existence precede essence?

Do we create our essence?

What am I?

Where am I?

What is our mind?

What is the Self?

Am I the "I"?

What else might I be?

SECTION II: *"QUESTIONS ABOUT YOU AND YOUR SPIRIT"*

Where does the Spirit exist?

What is the spirit's lifespan?

What is the mind-body problem?

Do the mind, body, and spirit interact?

Is consciousness our existence?

Are we a Happening?

Do We Have a Conscience?

SECTION III: *"QUESTIONS ABOUT YOUR IDENTITY"*

How stable and changeable am I?

How do I become more stable?

How free am I?

How much are other people part of my identity?

How much do I share an identity with a supreme being?

How much does my identity change from time to time?

How much do I want to change?

SECTION IV: *"TRUTH AND KNOWLEDGE"*

How much do I trust my senses?

How much do I trust reasoning?

How much do I trust science?

How much do I trust in my conscience or inner self/spirit?

How much do I trust general abstractions?

How much do I trust knowledge from experiential living?

SECTION V: *"CHOICES YOU CAN MAKE ABOUT YOUR BEING"*

I am a material being similar to all others and/or Am a unique spirit

I am determined by heredity and environment and/or I am a free agent.

I live to maximize personal pleasure and/or I live to find meaning.

Personal change occurs gradually in steps and/or I can change in a short time.

Understanding the self and others is a science and/or Understanding the self is an art.

Understanding self requires analysis and/or Understanding is a creative act.

SECTION VI: *"CHOICES ABOUT UNDERSTANDING OTHERS"*

Focus on causal background and/or Focus on the present and spirit.

Trust in intellect and reasoning and/or Trust feelings/conscience.

Believe truth is relative/unknowable and/or Believe absolutes can be known.

Utilize only the best method for knowing and/or utilize all ways of knowing.

Use laws for understanding and/or insights for understanding.

SECTION VII: *"CHOICES ABOUT YOUR RELATIONSHIP WITH OTHERS"*

Change others and/or accept others as they are.

Focus on tolerance and/or Focus on love.

Seek service and/or Give service.

Use high power when relating and/or Use low power when relating

Retain past and/or Forgive

Label and categorize others and/or Be non-judgmental.

Use others to achieve success and/or Help others succeed.

Expect Only Correct Perspective and/or Respect Other's Perspectives

Educate for behavior change and/or Educate the heart and spirit

Teach correct perspective and/or Build upon the perspective of others

Withdraw when non-rewarding and/or Care for others indefinitely

Summary of Choices

About the Authors

SECTION I: *"QUESTIONS ABOUT YOUR EXISTENCE"*

There is a special area of philosophy/psychology that deals with self-betrayal and self-deception. For theorists in these areas, the idea that people do not know themselves, or betray their true selves, is, unfortunately, all too common. These theorists believe that this self-betrayal or deception leads to tragic living with dishonesty and misunderstanding in human relationships and loss of freedom to be your true self. Don't worry; you won't be drug into those long and tedious existential discourses about self-betrayal here.

Is There Another World?

About the material world be wise,

You must face it to survive.

You can put the spiritual aside.

But then you won't be fully alive.

Truth be told, there are as many worlds as there are people. We all start out biologically different and then we all have different experiences. From these differences, we learn to perceive the world differently. In doing so we each create our own worldviews and thus it just logically follows that l we all live in different worlds.

But the conglomerate of all these individual worlds falls somewhere between seeing things through spiritual eyes and/or interpreting life more with worldly materialistic eyes. Thus, a need to focus on both material and spiritual worldviews.

REFLECTIONS

We invite you to use this space to record your reflections, feelings, and insights. May this experience deepen your self-understanding and connection with others.

_____
_____
_____
_____
_____
_____
_____
_____
_____
_____
_____
_____
_____
_____
_____
_____
_____
_____
_____
_____
_____
_____
_____
_____
_____
_____
_____
_____
_____

Living In a World with More Wonder

When you see the spirit in another

You can more about yourself discover.

Because your own spirit, you will uncover

And then live with more wonder.

Actually, every perception we have lies somewhere on a continuum between the material and the spiritual. You have likely seen someone who views everything through a very materialistic prism and a contrasting person who embraces and interprets everything in a spiritual way. This awareness is a useful way to understand people. However, between the extremes each of us vacillates along the line between spiritual and material; back and forth depending on the topic, age, and recent experiences. The practical value of distinguishing where we are on the continuum between the spiritual world and the material world will become apparent later in this book.

REFLECTIONS

We invite you to use this space to record your reflections, feelings, and insights. May this experience deepen your self-understanding and connection with others.

_____
_____
_____
_____
_____
_____
_____
_____
_____
_____
_____
_____
_____
_____
_____
_____
_____
_____
_____
_____
_____
_____
_____
_____
_____
_____
_____
_____
_____

Am I More Than Brain Activity?

What am I, just brain activity?

That's not true,

There is something more.

About me and you.

Neuroscience finds that millions of connections in the brain are constantly changing as they respond to continuous sensory inputs. The inputs arrive from both external and internal signals. Thus, our consciousness, awareness, or essence is inevitably being created each moment by our continued living. The brain, just like the body, is the vehicle that enables our identity, our being, to evolve. This fact allows the possibility for the neuroscientist's knowledge of the brain to be compatible with a belief in free agency which will be discussed later.

REFLECTIONS

We invite you to use this space to record your reflections, feelings, and insights. May this experience deepen your self-understanding and connection with others.

_____
_____
_____
_____
_____
_____
_____
_____
_____
_____
_____
_____
_____
_____
_____
_____
_____
_____
_____
_____
_____
_____
_____
_____
_____
_____
_____
_____
_____

Does Existence Precede Essence?

Are we conscious?

Of our consciousness?

We know we exist.

But where and how do we exist?

One of the most serious criticisms of modern thought is that a person is most often considered to be a material object liken to everything else. But is there more to a person than protons and electrons to be analyzed into smaller and smaller less significant parts? The voices of existential philosophers from Kierkegaard, Heidegger, and Satre have proposed that humans cannot be adequately understood this way. The notion of the famous saying "existence precedes essence" leads us to the belief that a person first exists, which is our existence, and then the person creates his/her essence. In this book, I interpret this key statement in a way to present a positive, hopeful conclusion for you to contemplate.

This statement of existence precedes essence is interpreted here as that each human begins with an existence and then each creates or develops an essence. The essence is what we become; it is us, it is our consciousness, our awareness, it is really what we are as we live each day. We create our essence from our choices, perceptions, and reactions during our everyday experiences.

REFLECTIONS

We invite you to use this space to record your reflections, feelings, and insights. May this experience deepen your self-understanding and connection with others.

_____
_____
_____
_____
_____
_____
_____
_____
_____
_____
_____
_____
_____
_____
_____
_____
_____
_____
_____
_____
_____
_____
_____
_____
_____
_____
_____
_____
_____
_____

Do We Create Our Essence?

See me now.

I'll be changing somehow.

I'll be evolving.

I'll be a, 'HAPPENING.'

Now, among the existentialists who propose existence precedes essence there are differences in interpretation of 'existence precedes existence.' Some like Satre say there is no basic human nature, but more recent writers take another concept of self and propose we are born with innate self-growth tendencies. Obviously, we do first exist with the potential to think and have consciousness, awareness, and biological dispositions when perceiving our world.

Then, over time, we create ourselves or our essence. We change, evolve, develop, and grow. We are a 'Happening' and this is our ever-changing essence. We are always in the process of changing. Take your best guess about what you started with in your beginning existence and then look at what you created and became while living, which is your essence. You make your essence by your actions and choices. So now is the time to answer elusive questions about yourself.

REFLECTIONS

We invite you to use this space to record your reflections, feelings, and insights. May this experience deepen your self-understanding and connection with others.

_____
_____
_____
_____
_____
_____
_____
_____
_____
_____
_____
_____
_____
_____
_____
_____
_____
_____
_____
_____
_____
_____
_____
_____
_____
_____
_____
_____

What Am I?

The psychologist, the neuroscientist

They can explain the brain.

Yet you, your consciousness

They can't explain.

The popular belief is that the mind exists in the brain. However, the thing we call consciousness seems to be separate from any material entity. Furthermore, this entity, called consciousness or mind, seems to be extremely difficult to comprehend in terms of physical matter. We have not progressed much further from the statement: "I think therefore I am.

But this thinking, this choosing, has always been a staple, central part of human understanding throughout the centuries. Government, social society, and personal relationships all rest on perceiving that each person is directing and energizing one's acting. Each is deemed responsible for his/her actions, The most common, almost universal belief, is that within each individual is a thought, an intention, a Will, possibly a spirit, or a consciousness that directs and motivates human behavior.

REFLECTIONS

We invite you to use this space to record your reflections, feelings, and insights. May this experience deepen your self-understanding and connection with others.

_____
_____
_____
_____
_____
_____
_____
_____
_____
_____
_____
_____
_____
_____
_____
_____
_____
_____
_____
_____
_____
_____
_____
_____
_____
_____
_____
_____

Where Am I?

Our music exists outside the radio.

Where ideas exist, we really don't know.

Do we exist outside our brains?

Where we exist is hard to explain.

Where are you when you see the world?

Where are you when you see your past?

Where are you when you see your body?

Oh where, oh where, can you be.

There is a most important question, a most important question for this book, and a most important question for your life. Simply put, you must know what you are if you want to truly understand your life. The first clue to address this problem is revealed by another question: "Where do you exist?" There is one hundred percent agreement that each person is known to be identified by a body that is made of material that can be reduced to smaller and smaller units such as protons and electrons that can be located. But awareness, thinking, consciousness, and ideas are not material matters. Where do they exist?

REFLECTIONS

We invite you to use this space to record your reflections, feelings, and insights. May this experience deepen your self-understanding and connection with others.

_____
_____
_____
_____
_____
_____
_____
_____
_____
_____
_____
_____
_____
_____
_____
_____
_____
_____
_____
_____
_____
_____
_____
_____
_____
_____
_____
_____

What Is Our Mind?

Centuries ago, Descartes said,

"I think therefore I am."

Centuries ago, John Milton said,

"The mind is owned by the Self."

Yet in this century

The mind is still a mystery.

The Id, Ego, and Super-Ego were Freud's way of describing entities that existed inside of us at the closing of the nineteenth century. In the early twentieth century behavioral psychologists rejected Freud's theory and replaced it with another that proposed it was unscientific and unnecessary to believe in some entity inside of us like the mind. Instead, they proposed that classical and operant conditioning was sufficient to explain behavior; no mind was required.

Know thyself", "To thine own self be true", "Just be yourself". These are a sampling of the advice you have undoubtedly heard about gaining self-understanding. Why must we consciously work to accomplish the obvious? Who else could you be and aren't you always aware of just who you are, who else would know you better if you were with yourself 24 hours, each and every day?

REFLECTIONS

We invite you to use this space to record your reflections, feelings, and insights. May this experience deepen your self-understanding and connection with others.

_____
_____
_____
_____
_____
_____
_____
_____
_____
_____
_____
_____
_____
_____
_____
_____
_____
_____
_____
_____
_____
_____
_____
_____
_____
_____
_____
_____

What Is The Self?

Today they try to tell us.

Our brain is our mind.

But better explanations

You can find.

Freud liked Ego,

Theologians like Spirit,

Psychologists like Self,

All are trying to be explaining our existence.

The word Self is used to describe an entity within the person that directs behavior. The Self was usually described as being the product of innate perceptual processes and environmental inputs primarily from significant others. This focus on the self leads to the excellent research of a past President of the American Psychological Association, Albert Bandura. His internal agents are Self-Efficacy and Self-Regulation, which come closest to fitting well with the popular conception of the mind or consciousness.

REFLECTIONS

We invite you to use this space to record your reflections, feelings, and insights. May this experience deepen your self-understanding and connection with others.

_____
_____
_____
_____
_____
_____
_____
_____
_____
_____
_____
_____
_____
_____
_____
_____
_____
_____
_____
_____
_____
_____
_____
_____
_____
_____
_____
_____

Am I The 'I'?

So, what am I; am I the elusive 'I'?

We hear the words; "I thought, I cried, I tried.

We hear; "I choose, I refuse, I will, I feel."

Well, whatever I am; I am real.

The word ego when translated means Ick or 'I' in the German language. In most theories about the mind, consciousness, and existence there is, within us, a material or an undetected hypothetical variable that is thought to exist. Scientists call such a thing an "intervening variable." They believe in something not directly observable, which is necessary to understand a phenomenon. Thus came the agreeable resolution to give that something within us the name; "I."

In the popular vernacular, the common language, the popular most straightforward, and parsimonious name is; 'I`. This conclusion is based on most explanations of human thinking and behavior. Notice that new theories are similar to the century-old theological belief in the existence of a spirit which is intertwined with the body to explain human consciousness and existence.

REFLECTIONS

We invite you to use this space to record your reflections, feelings, and insights. May this experience deepen your self-understanding and connection with others.

_____
_____
_____
_____
_____
_____
_____
_____
_____
_____
_____
_____
_____
_____
_____
_____
_____
_____
_____
_____
_____
_____
_____
_____
_____
_____
_____

What Else Might I Be?

You may not even sense it.

Skeptics will reject it.

Scientists forget it.

It is that thing called Spirit.

They say this about the Spirit.

If you can't observe it

Then don't accept it.

Forget it.

You might ask yourself if you are just the body with a brain. Or are you also a Spirit? Obviously, the Spirit is said to accompany the body and act in unison. So, is it, not a serious omission to discount centuries of including and believing that humans have a Spirit? In fact, if the Spirit is that part of a being that exists in a timeless way, both before and after death, then the Spirit is the most important part of a human. It does not make sense to leave it out of our considerations here.

REFLECTIONS

We invite you to use this space to record your reflections, feelings, and insights. May this experience deepen your self-understanding and connection with others.

_____
_____
_____
_____
_____
_____
_____
_____
_____
_____
_____
_____
_____
_____
_____
_____
_____
_____
_____
_____
_____
_____
_____
_____
_____
_____

SECTION II: *"QUESTIONS ABOUT YOU AND YOUR SPIRIT"*

Instead, the focus in this book will be on you. Answer directly with your feelings about who you are, your identity, nature of being, understanding of others, and the way you want to relate with others. Again, for most of these questions, you have already formed some opinions, but you may want to reconsider and improve your answers for the purpose of choosing a better way to live. Just proceed by answering the questions with feelings as well as intellect.

Where Does The Spirit Exist?

The spirit is said to be part of us.

But what does it mean if it can't be seen?

Did it before we existed?

Does it after we exist?

And does it reside inside?

Or does it remain outside?

And is it influencing,

Choosing, what we are doing.

You might, as many others, want to add a third element to the question of, "What am I?" Most people now and in the past believe that combined with the body and the mind is a spirit. Christianity, Islam, and most religions believe that a spirit exists as part of the person, or the person is or has a spirit. Usually, the spirit is believed to exist before, during, and after the life of the body and possibly the mind. This spirit is typically thought to exist in a timeless way.

REFLECTIONS

We invite you to use this space to record your reflections, feelings, and insights. May this experience deepen your self-understanding and connection with others.

_____
_____
_____
_____
_____
_____
_____
_____
_____
_____
_____
_____
_____
_____
_____
_____
_____
_____
_____
_____
_____
_____
_____
_____
_____
_____
_____
_____

What Is The Spirit's Lifespan?

When do we end?

Surely your body will die.

But like most others, we persist

Believing we will forever exist.

Even non-religious scholarship often refers to man's Spirit. In common language we say such things as "He has a mean Spirit", "Don't break the boys' Spirit", and "You have a good Spirit", If you believe that each person has a Spirit and the Spirit has an enduring eternal quality then everything you conclude about yourself and others will be different. If the Spirit endures after the body, then isn't it just logical to conclude that the Spirit is the central or key enduring feature of the person you are now creating?

REFLECTIONS

We invite you to use this space to record your reflections, feelings, and insights. May this experience deepen your self-understanding and connection with others.

_____
_____
_____
_____
_____
_____
_____
_____
_____
_____
_____
_____
_____
_____
_____
_____
_____
_____
_____
_____
_____
_____
_____
_____
_____
_____
_____
_____
_____
_____
_____
_____

What Is The Mind-Body Problem?

Mind and body,

Only one can be seen.

But the unseen seems

To reign supreme.

So, does the mind direct the body?

Does the body own the mind?

Eventually, you are sure to find

They work together all the time.

For centuries philosophers and scientists have faced what is called the mind-body problem. How do the mind and body influence one another, and what is the function of each? Even after centuries of debate, no consensus has been reached, and thus this failure leads to another question you should answer for yourself. The first consideration is a matter of time and space. Is the mind and spirit housed within the body and if so, is it or are they both limited to this space? Would the existence of mind and spirit depend upon the existence of the body? There is certainly hard evidence that the body influences the mind; especially that part of the body called the brain. Without question the body influences the mind and the mind influences the body. What about the spirit?

REFLECTIONS

We invite you to use this space to record your reflections, feelings, and insights. May this experience deepen your self-understanding and connection with others.

_____
_____
_____
_____
_____
_____
_____
_____
_____
_____
_____
_____
_____
_____
_____
_____
_____
_____
_____
_____
_____
_____
_____
_____
_____
_____
_____
_____

Do The Mind, Body, And Spirit Interact?

For that something called Spirit

They have words to replace it.

Mind, awareness, ego, and self

If not these then something else.

For those who believe that the person consists of a body, mind, and/or spirit the question of functional roles is indeed complex. The spirit is seen to be the enduring component rather than the body. Or should the focus then be on the spirit? If so, do the body and the mind influence the spirit? From an influence perspective it is equally important to ask the question, "Does the spirit influence the body and the mind?"

The question of whether the mind influences the body is generally accepted, almost as a premise, that the mind is central in directing and energizing the behavior of the body. Furthermore, the mind seems to be closely related to physical health. We are far from being able to fully appreciate the interaction of these three entities. But let us try to do our best to at least clarify the possibilities.

REFLECTIONS

We invite you to use this space to record your reflections, feelings, and insights. May this experience deepen your self-understanding and connection with others.

_____
_____
_____
_____
_____
_____
_____
_____
_____
_____
_____
_____
_____
_____
_____
_____
_____
_____
_____
_____
_____
_____
_____
_____
_____
_____
_____
_____

Is Consciousness Our Existence?

My brain will someday be dying.

And then will I be nothing?

Not thinking,

Not even existing?

We know we exist,

We call it consciousness.

We don't know if it's outside or inside of us.

But it's there, somewhere, you can trust.

Philosophers, psychologists, and behavior scientists have almost always postulated that there is some intervening variable between the external world (stimulus) and the behavior of an individual person (response). Again, consider the names they have given such as consciousness, awareness, self, and ego. A past President of the American Psychological Association, Albert Bandura centered his theory around the phrase, "Self-Efficacy" which he defined as the capacity of the Self to exert control over motivation, well-being, and personal behavior. Other psychologists refer to Self-Monitoring, Self, Self-Concept, Self -Esteem, Self-Regard, Self- Control. Over and over the word Self is used to refer to something inside the person.

REFLECTIONS

We invite you to use this space to record your reflections, feelings, and insights. May this experience deepen your self-understanding and connection with others.

_____

_____

_____

_____

_____

_____

_____

_____

_____

_____

_____

_____

_____

_____

_____

_____

_____

_____

_____

_____

_____

_____

_____

_____

_____

_____

_____

Are We A Happening?

Can I, do I, choose what I want to be?

Our Spirit gives us this possibility.

By shaping and creating

An ever-changing me.

Call it what you will, but it is very useful, common, and natural to believe there is some kind of agent within you. Freud named the Id, ego, and superego, theologians identify a spirit, and hundreds of psychologists use multiple terms. The most popular is the Self. Existentialists imply there is more to us than corpus when they prioritize all this choosing. The practicality of believing in an inner self is demonstrated in innumerable research studies. It is one of the most researched topics in scientific psychology journals.

One way to answer this is to say that a person is not an object but a 'Happening'. The unified person is never a static object but something that is continually evolving, unfolding, and changing. In this conception, the person cannot be separated from the environment and certainly not from others with whom the person is changing. Progression will always be part of our definition and understanding of each Happening or what we call a person.

REFLECTIONS

We invite you to use this space to record your reflections, feelings, and insights. May this experience deepen your self-understanding and connection with others.

_____
_____
_____
_____
_____
_____
_____
_____
_____
_____
_____
_____
_____
_____
_____
_____
_____
_____
_____
_____
_____
_____
_____
_____
_____
_____
_____
_____
_____
_____

Do We Have A Conscience?

Some beliefs are stronger and last longer.

They are those within our conscience.

They always seem to have a presence.

They are the core of our essence.

Throughout the centuries the writings of men refer to a conscience. Sometimes it has been called moral sensitivity, an inner knowledge, or a voice that identifies right and wrong, good, and bad. In the twentieth century, it has been associated with religion, but even secular humanists refer to conscience as do political and social theorists. It seems to be a distinct and universal attribute of the human and we call it conscience.

Perhaps some of the more interesting explanations of conscience or something like conscience have been made by social biologists. In the writings of E.O. Wilson, the evolutionary biologist, there is an excellent account of how moral sensitivity or altruism has a genetic basis that improves reproductive fitness. In most cases, the explanations, such as those given by the social biologist, and some philosophers, refer to something as innate and inherited. Conscience is thus seen as part of our basic makeup as humans.

REFLECTIONS

We invite you to use this space to record your reflections, feelings, and insights. May this experience deepen your self-understanding and connection with others.

_____
_____
_____
_____
_____
_____
_____
_____
_____
_____
_____
_____
_____
_____
_____
_____
_____
_____
_____
_____
_____
_____
_____
_____
_____
_____
_____
_____

SECTION III: *"QUESTIONS ABOUT YOUR IDENTITY"*

How stable and changeable am I?

How do I become more stable?

How free am I?

How much are other people a part of my identity?

How much do I share an identity with a supreme being?

How much does my identity change from time to time?

How much do I want to change?

Now that you have encountered some views about the nature of your existence, you are better able to examine your essence. Most of the existentialists who believe "existence precedes essence" take this view because they believe we create our essence by choosing, acting, or just being in the world.

Of course, we can't choose, or be whatever we want for we are restricted or limited by our body and environment. This is a fact and is called in existential writings' facticity. But at any present moment, in time, we can, with our facticity, choose to make ourselves, to be self-creating beings. We are not an object solely shaped by a determining past. Instead, we are free and choose our future being. The past informs us about our facticity but does not determine our essence. Life is always moving forward and each person is part of the ever-changing flow forward. So our essence or identity, what we are, is always in a state of forward movement and results from our choices.

How Stable And Changeable Am I?

It is good to be stable and predictable.

But changing is inevitable, even desirable.

Changing makes us flexible and sensible.

So, we need both stable and changeable to be reliable.

Decades ago, in the twentieth century, it was popular for psychology departments to offer a course on individual differences. When teaching this course, I used a book entitled *Stability and Change in Human Characteristics,* by Benjamin Bloom. In general, we act as if each individual were a stable material object. However, whenever much reflection is given to this question the answer is in the opposite direction. You and I and all people are found to change during the life course, during the year, during the day, and even each moment. Is it more useful to conclude that in understanding people we are dealing with constantly changing entities, not stable objects?

We usually think that changes in the mind influence the body, but we know that bodily changes dramatically alter the mind and possibly the spirit. Those who seem to know most about the spirit point out that the spirit also changes. Expressions as: "Her spirit soared," "My Spirit was strong that day," and "The experience seemed to have broken his spirit," all attest to the fact that people's spirits range from strong and vibrant to seemingly nonexistence for a period of time. Differences in spirit are said to vary from person to person, and within the person from time to time and place to place. Whenever this happens, are people changed?

REFLECTIONS

We invite you to use this space to record your reflections, feelings, and insights. May this experience deepen your self-understanding and connection with others.

_____

_____

_____

_____

_____

_____

_____

_____

_____

_____

_____

_____

_____

_____

_____

_____

_____

_____

_____

_____

_____

_____

_____

_____

_____

_____

_____

_____

_____

_____

_____

How Do I Become More Stable?

Where is the anchor for my stability?

Is it following my conscience's reliability?

It is my most important responsibility.

It is the anchor for my stability.

I must share at this time my belief in one of the most important but almost totally overlooked dynamics that help us understand how we exist. It is the relative strength of our spirit to our body at any moment in time. You might understand this by noting b that the body is constantly changing based on nutrition, energy, rest, stimulation, circumstance, training, etc. The body can be weak, strong, active, passive, and constantly changing. It is less obvious but equally plausible that the mind and spirit may also have these same characteristics. If so, then what a person is at any moment is a complicated give-and-take interplay between a dynamic vacillating and changing body, mind, and spirit and they all act together as a unity to produce at each moment a person, a different person, a unique person, a Happening.

In life, we constantly try to find stability and fortunately, there is stability. But why are some people more stable than others and to what do you attribute your stability? Maybe people vary greatly in the extent to which either their biochemistry, mind, or spirit give them stability. Other sources of stability could include being responsible to others, feeling responsible to God, or living according to one's conscience. This is an extremely important question so do your best to examine an answer for yourself.

REFLECTIONS

We invite you to use this space to record your reflections, feelings, and insights. May this experience deepen your self-understanding and connection with others.

_____
_____
_____
_____
_____
_____
_____
_____
_____
_____
_____
_____
_____
_____
_____
_____
_____
_____
_____
_____
_____
_____
_____
_____
_____
_____
_____
_____

How Free Am I?

We are only free

In a way we want to be

When with our conscience

We live in precious harmony.

In our society, the core question of political, economic, legal, and metaphysical philosophy is the question of freedom. It is also an obsession among the general population to be personally free. While this question may not be as important those who just answered the freedom question will not go away. So, at this time I would like you to answer the question: "How free am I?"

The question of freedom, however, does depend on the definition of freedom. Often freedom is associated with the term agency referring to the belief that people are free agents. In the usual way of thinking freedom refers to having the conditions and opportunity to say and do as one pleases. Another definition refers to the ability to make choices. A more profound and deep understanding of freedom has to do with how you live. Are some ways of living the key to being free? In this last way of defining freedom, it is how you live that determines the true and honest experience of human freedom. In the simplest terms, it defines freedom as that state of being that occurs when living a life that is congruent with your true nature.

REFLECTIONS

We invite you to use this space to record your reflections, feelings, and insights. May this experience deepen your self-understanding and connection with others.

_____
_____
_____
_____
_____
_____
_____
_____
_____
_____
_____
_____
_____
_____
_____
_____
_____
_____
_____
_____
_____
_____
_____
_____
_____
_____
_____
_____

How Much Are Other People Part Of My Identity?

Man is a social creature,

Understood only in the face of another.

Our identities are not singular.

They are shared together.

A mother bear with a cub is a different animal from the same mother bear without a cub. I have been surprised at my bravery when I have had to protect my children. The expression "no man is an island" is especially true when talking about identity. Thus, if you want to understand yourself, you must also consider how you define yourself with significant others. A mother is an almost perfect example of this. Even before birth, her baby has become part of her, and her identity does not now exist apart from her child. Mother and child share, in the course of living, their identity with one another. The mother does not exist separately from the child. This is sometimes true of husband and wife, or even sometimes of soldiers in the same unit. A consequence or outcome for one person is a consequence and outcome for the other. Indeed, people whom I would categorize as having a shared identity readily state that when an honor is bestowed on the other it is as if they had received it themselves or if the other suffered, they suffered too.

Furthermore, there have been changes in existential thought that point out we are not just objects, but we exist in relationships with the environment, the culture, and most importantly with others. Martin Heidegger emphasizes that humans, being-in-the-world, are embedded and cannot be extracted from meaningful social interactions.

REFLECTIONS

We invite you to use this space to record your reflections, feelings, and insights. May this experience deepen your self-understanding and connection with others.

_____

_____

_____

_____

_____

_____

_____

_____

_____

_____

_____

_____

_____

_____

_____

_____

_____

_____

_____

_____

_____

_____

_____

_____

_____

_____

_____

_____

_____

_____

How Much Do I Share An Identity
With A Supreme Being?

Words about God will intrude

Into our lives repeatedly.

And when we respond, be it kind or rude,

God becomes part of our identity.

On the surface, it appears that some men seem to think little about God. A supreme being seems to have no part in their life. But that may not be a complete and accurate picture. Is there for such persons a latent concern or awareness of God that is never activated until circumstances evoke dormant knowledge? I do not know the answer to this question, but I am well aware of public opinion polls, survey data, and historical documentation confirming that people have through the centuries, worldwide, expressed not only an interest but proclaimed a knowledge of God.

God is understood in terms of their own lives. The ancient Greeks, for example, prayed to God, sacrificed, and asked for favors from their distant, non-loving, and not-so-admirable gods. This relationship with God is also present in a modern Christian who states, on the contrary, that God the Father is a kind heavenly parent who has personal love and concern for each of us. In such a case it is easy to see how God, who is also a father, is involved daily in one's life and thus becomes part of a person's identity. Their inclusion of God as part of their identity thus involves their beliefs, desires, what they think about, and the choices they make.

REFLECTIONS

We invite you to use this space to record your reflections, feelings, and insights. May this experience deepen your self-understanding and connection with others.

_____
_____
_____
_____
_____
_____
_____
_____
_____
_____
_____
_____
_____
_____
_____
_____
_____
_____
_____
_____
_____
_____
_____
_____
_____
_____
_____
_____

How Much Does My Identity Change
From Time to Time?

"Trust me he'll never change".

"Trust me he won't change".

"Trust me you will change".

Change is inevitable

Change is desirable.

"He became an entirely different person when he moved to California." "He was never that way as a child." Such statements about change are buttressed by the whole field of developmental psychology. Change in this academic discipline is the one constant in understanding human behavior. It is not really a matter of whether we change but possibly how much we change why, when, and where.

Return for a moment to a previous discussion where we noted that a change in one's bodily state, such as going from sickness to health, or from drug use to sober influences both mind and/or spirit. There are also some contexts or situations where there are extreme and pronounced effects simultaneously on body, mind, and spirit.

The greatest changes in your identity are those associated with changes in space and time which are of course inevitable. Great dramatic changes come from your identification, relationships, and interactions with significant others including praying to a God. Religious writings are replete with total transformations seen in the individuals who report that God came into their lives. History is filled with dramatic accounts of personal transformations.

REFLECTIONS

We invite you to use this space to record your reflections, feelings, and insights. May this experience deepen your self-understanding and connection with others.

_____
_____
_____
_____
_____
_____
_____
_____
_____
_____
_____
_____
_____
_____
_____
_____
_____
_____
_____
_____
_____
_____
_____
_____
_____
_____
_____
_____

How Much Do You Want to Change?

Inevitably we will change.

And our lives will rearrange.

To resist, even a little,

Is impossible and futile.

It might seem paradoxical, but perhaps those who are most satisfied with their present identity are also those who welcome more change in their identity. The truth of this may be seen in the converse where those who are most dissatisfied are those who are most defensive and protective of themselves and most fearful of change. Again, you may see my bias about the best answer to this question. However, how much you want to change is an important question for it has direct applications for what will happen to you in the future. If you do not want to change then it is likely that your eventual inevitable change will be different than what you want even though you may try to prevent it. If you welcome change in your identity then you can take a most active role in determining the direction and amount of change. Regardless, you will change.

The essential point is that by welcoming change you have a better chance of participating and creating your future identity which will, of course, be different anyway than what it is today. These considerations may influence your answer to how much you welcome and accept change.

REFLECTIONS

We invite you to use this space to record your reflections, feelings, and insights. May this experience deepen your self-understanding and connection with others.

_____
_____
_____
_____
_____
_____
_____
_____
_____
_____
_____
_____
_____
_____
_____
_____
_____
_____
_____
_____
_____
_____
_____
_____
_____
_____
_____
_____

SECTION IV: *"QUESTIONS TO ANSWER ABOUT TRUTH AND KNOWLEDGE"*

How much do I trust my senses?

How much do I trust reasoning?

How much do I trust science?

How much do I trust in my conscience or inner self/spirit?

How much do I trust general abstractions?

How much do I trust knowledge from experiential living?

(literature, media, introspection, observations, traditions, case studies, personal interactions, intuition, etc.)?

How Much Do I Trust My Senses?

What we see, hear, or feel can be in error.

Yet, we will rely on them forever.

Reason must come to the rescue.

To help us find just what is true.

"Seeing is believing," or "I'd have to first see that" are two phrases commonly associated with the belief that the most certain knowledge is that which we can hear or see. However, anyone acquainted with nineteenth-century philosophy or psychology will find that the sensations that come to the eye or ear can be misleading. They are often perceived differently and riddled with distortion, even error. The popularity and skill of the magician are based on the fact that our perceptions do not give us certain knowledge of what has taken place. Repeatedly our senses deceive us. Bertrand Russell, when writing about a table, shows how the color, texture, and shape of a table may be very different than what we perceive visually, and yet we always know it to be a table.

We usually admire the man who says, "Show me or prove it to me first." Prove it usually means providing sensory evidence. And yet, there are many times in our existence when we must act without this kind of knowledge to survive and prosper. We need to trust others. We need to make conclusions based on reasoning, and circumstantial evidence. We need to be aware that our feelings and reasoning also guide us to appropriate actions with our fellow human beings.

REFLECTIONS

We invite you to use this space to record your reflections, feelings, and insights. May this experience deepen your self-understanding and connection with others.

_____
_____
_____
_____
_____
_____
_____
_____
_____
_____
_____
_____
_____
_____
_____
_____
_____
_____
_____
_____
_____
_____
_____
_____
_____
_____
_____

How Much Do I Trust Reasoning?

Sometimes we make decisions based on facts.

Sometimes we make decisions based on reason.

However, a good decision

Needs both facts and reason.

It is useful to consider two types of reasoning. The first is scientific reasoning which has for its basis sensory data. The other kind of reasoning has for its basis fundamental propositions that seem to be infallible and from these acceptable premises, we proceed with formal or informal mental calculations. Supposedly this brings us knowledge and truth. It must be obvious to you that the conclusions reached through the most careful and astute reasoning can be no better than the propositions upon which they rest.

In the case of scientific reasoning, the conclusions will be wrong if the sensory data is incorrect. As for the other kinds of reasoning, the conclusions will also be false if the fundamental premise or propositions are in error. For example, if you began your reasoning with a fundamental belief that people are basically good or people are basically bad the conclusions reached would ordinarily be contradictory from the contradictory beginnings. Reasoning is a tool used to supplement and expand what may or may not be true beginnings. Furthermore, it can easily be shown that the mental calculations used in reasoning can lead to inaccurate conclusions through faulty reasoning. These kinds of problems in reasoning systems are continually demonstrated in introductory courses in logic.

REFLECTIONS

We invite you to use this space to record your reflections, feelings, and insights. May this experience deepen your self-understanding and connection with others.

_____

_____

_____

_____

_____

_____

_____

_____

_____

_____

_____

_____

_____

_____

_____

_____

_____

_____

_____

_____

_____

_____

_____

_____

_____

_____

_____

_____

_____

How Much Do I Trust Science?

My professor did pronounce,

"If anything exists, it exists in some amount."

Thus, what can't be measured must not exist

Yet our beliefs in unseen things persist.

Only what is observable,

Is scientifically acceptable.

Isn't there something missing here?

Yes, the very feelings we hold so dear.

The greatest, the most dramatic illustration of truth-finding in our modern culture is science. Everyone has to be impressed with the undeniable achievements of science in the physical world. And science is the foundation for truth and knowledge in our scientifically technically based society. However, you should be aware that honest scientists will tell you directly that they cannot and in fact do not want to use this method to tell you about the spiritual world. If you believe that people are more than a material body, then wisdom would dictate that you must turn to other methods to obtain more complete truth and knowledge about people. The truly honest scientist is a person who would say that his discipline provides limited and certainly incomplete information about the human spirit.

REFLECTIONS

We invite you to use this space to record your reflections, feelings, and insights. May this experience deepen your self-understanding and connection with others.

_____
_____
_____
_____
_____
_____
_____
_____
_____
_____
_____
_____
_____
_____
_____
_____
_____
_____
_____
_____
_____
_____
_____
_____
_____
_____
_____
_____
_____

How Much Do I Trust In My Conscience?

The difference between selfishness and

Goodness is not difficult to know.

Your conscience can tell you so.

People through all times and ages report that they are able to know about things from their conscience or inner spirit especially in matters of right and wrong, and good and bad. People who are devoted to this type of knowledge generally place it above all other forms of knowledge. Some people are so trusting and so dedicated to this knowledge, coming from one's conscience, that they will sometimes choose death rather than violate their conscience.

Living according to your conscience is a solid foundation for living free. Again, one must first ask to what extent a person has a conscience. It is rooted in feelings as well as intellect. The problem with this kind of knowledge is that it does not give the same answers to all people. Can this problem be resolved?

One straightforward answer is that what is absolutely right for person 'A' may be absolutely wrong for person 'B' based on differences in the person's perceptions, experiences, and circumstances. This is sometimes called context and is not to be confused with relativism. This does not mean that there is no absolute truth and that everything is relative to each person's conscience. But each person receives an assurance that they are acting according to their conscience even though the answer may not be the same as that of someone else. This indeed is a complex question with which you are faced. But to live free you must come to terms with your own conscience.

REFLECTIONS

We invite you to use this space to record your reflections, feelings, and insights. May this experience deepen your self-understanding and connection with others.

_____
_____
_____
_____
_____
_____
_____
_____
_____
_____
_____
_____
_____
_____
_____
_____
_____
_____
_____
_____
_____
_____
_____
_____
_____
_____
_____

How Much Do I Trust General Abstractions And Rules?

Who knows you best?

It's not the psychiatrist.

Here's the real test.

It's someone you lived with.

How much you trust general abstractions will usually depend upon whether you see and find alternative ways to know about things and persons. The alternative to general abstractions and /or rules is direct personal knowledge based on concrete experience. This distinction is particularly applicable to understanding self and others and needs to be clarified

In my classes, throughout the years, I always asked my students, "Who knows you best?" Never has anyone said their therapist or counselor. Almost always they say their mother, sometimes their father, or a sibling, sometimes their spouse. Notice that the trusted people are those with whom the person has shared their life. They are not people who are particularly astute at understanding and knowing laws and abstractions about human behavior. They are people who have served, lived, and shared a world together. How artificial it is to try and understand someone in an office. To best understand another person, you need to do things like eat together, work on a job, share stories, take care of one another when sick, or live with them in a loving, serving, unselfish way. Does this not tell you about the way to truly understand self and others?

REFLECTIONS

We invite you to use this space to record your reflections, feelings, and insights. May this experience deepen your self-understanding and connection with others.

_____
_____
_____
_____
_____
_____
_____
_____
_____
_____
_____
_____
_____
_____
_____
_____
_____
_____
_____
_____
_____
_____
_____
_____
_____
_____
_____
_____
_____

How Much Do I Trust Knowledge
From Experiential Living?

There is no better way of learning

Than just plain living and being.

It happens every day when thinking and feeling.

Philosophers call it experiential living.

There is a kind of knowledge that comes from experiential living. This is the kind of living we all do from infancy to death. We live and interact with objects and other people. We learn from meeting them and accepting them in a way in which they become part of our experiential world. By experiential world I refer to the way that we interpret the everyday objects, events, and people as they appear to us and as they present themselves to us. It truly is informal learning, but perhaps it is the most important type of learning that brings about an understanding of others and ourselves.

These interactions and learning gradually accumulate to tell us much about who we are and tell us about the people we live with. We come to know them directly, but we also acquire certain abstractions and concepts about what people are like. Some are much better attuned, interested, and intellectually capable of benefiting from this kind of learning. Often such people share what they have learned with us. Thus, we learn from one another and from our own experiences a type of truth and knowledge that is unequaled and irreplaceable when it comes to understanding self and others. So, to what extent do you value this everyday experiential information, knowledge, and truth?

REFLECTIONS

We invite you to use this space to record your reflections, feelings, and insights. May this experience deepen your self-understanding and connection with others.

_____
_____
_____
_____
_____
_____
_____
_____
_____
_____
_____
_____
_____
_____
_____
_____
_____
_____
_____
_____
_____
_____
_____
_____
_____
_____
_____
_____
_____

SECTION V: "CHOICES YOU CAN MAKE ABOUT YOUR BEING"

I am a material being similar to all others	*and/or Am a unique spirit*
I am determined by heredity and environment	*and/or I am a free agent*
I live to maximize personal pleasure	*and/or I live to find meaning*
Personal change occurs gradually in steps	*and/or I can change in a short time*
Understanding the self and others is a science art	*and/or Am a unique spirit*

Before proceeding further an explanation needs to be made of the use of the word choices. Ordinarily, a choice is between opposites something good and bad, desirable and undesirable, etc. What you will find in this section is that choices are often found between two things that are good or two things that are true. Sometimes there's clearly one that is better, but the other also has merit. Sometimes the choice is a compromise between the two. Perhaps one way to regard these choices is to call them an emphasis rather than a choice where two seemingly opposites are presented. It may be that sometimes you want to emphasize one and at other times emphasize the other; or believe both and simply emphasize one.

It won't take you long to discover that I have a real preference for the second alternative in the choices to follow. My preference for the second alternative is not always reflected in my behavior for the first alternative is so often mandatory for success in the material world.

I Am A Material Being Similar To All Others
and/or
I Am A Unique Spirit

Recognize human commonalities.

But value unique personalities.

Same and different is what's meant to be.

And that's frustrating for you and me.

The first chapter of a psychology textbook will insist that psychology is a science. Each person is regarded as an entity consisting of a body and particular attention is paid to the brain for the purpose of understanding the general laws that regulate behavior. The laws are held to apply to all persons. Under this concept, you would be, like all others, subject to the same laws. But if each person is different in one or more unique ways, then that person should be studied as that type of person and the laws that govern that type of person would need to be applied. Thus, you and all people like you are to be studied objectively for the purpose of finding the principles controlling your behavior.

In contrast, this scientific approach, presented in almost all textbooks, is another way to view your being. It is that while having a body and brain generally similar to all other people you are distinct and unique because of your spirit, body, and mind. But the spirit, because it cannot be observed in public and in a repeated fashion is beyond the ability of scientists to study. This doesn't mean that your spirit does not exist. It simply means that psychology would not be able to consider you as a unique spirit. The choice here is quite clear and important.

REFLECTIONS

We invite you to use this space to record your reflections, feelings, and insights. May this experience deepen your self-understanding and connection with others.

_____
_____
_____
_____
_____
_____
_____
_____
_____
_____
_____
_____
_____
_____
_____
_____
_____
_____
_____
_____
_____
_____
_____
_____
_____
_____
_____
_____
_____
_____

I Am Determined By Heredity And Environment
and/or
I Am A Free Agent

Are we determined by heredity and environment,

And is believing so a scientific requirement?

Or are we free to believe we are free?

It's a crucial choice for you and me.

In psychology textbooks, you would be hard put to find a discussion of factors that influence behavior that were not considered as either part of hereditary or of the environment. While there are excellent discussions of cognition and mental processes there is always an underlying assumption that these cognitions are produced in the brain and regulated by the environment with hereditary implications imposed. Thus, whatever you are can be explained by heredity and environment.

In contrast, you may want to believe that you are a free agentic being. If you take this position, you could still believe that you are determined by heredity and environment. It is impossible to deny the research findings demonstrating heredity and environmental influences. I have not read one theorist that denies heredity and environment influences behavior and thought. However, there are many who believe that heredity and environment play a much smaller role in energizing and directing behavior. They believe that the person can be free in both action and thought and now the question is put to you.

REFLECTIONS

We invite you to use this space to record your reflections, feelings, and insights. May this experience deepen your self-understanding and connection with others.

_____
_____
_____
_____
_____
_____
_____
_____
_____
_____
_____
_____
_____
_____
_____
_____
_____
_____
_____
_____
_____
_____
_____
_____
_____
_____
_____

I Live to Maximize Personal Pleasure
and/or
I Live To Find Meaning In Life

You can find pleasure in seeking meaning

But not meaning from seeking pleasure.

From Freud's pleasure principle to B.F. Skinner's reinforcers, the driving force in motivation, are said to be a hedonistic personal pleasure. Almost all motivational and personality theorists believe the driving force in human action is some type of broadly defined pain reduction or pleasure. However, it certainly doesn't require a Ph.D. to know that men like pleasure and, like all animals, try to avoid pain. This fundamental truth has been known from day one and requires little time to recognize that each day you spend time trying to do more pleasurable things and want to spend less time doing things that are troublesome, painful, annoying, and frustrating. This is a true and correct principle or abstraction. It could even be considered a basic law of human behavior.

But we also know that sometimes we willingly accept a great deal of pain and difficulties to do something that we consider meaningful. A father puts up with much unpleasantness at the butcher shop in order to send his son to college. It is not hard to find examples of meaning trumping pain and pleasure. Both living to maximize pleasure and living to find meaning in life are true. descriptions of the human condition. They are opposites, but they are both operas in our lives. It is good to live a life pleasurable, even joyful, so it is a good principle as well as a true principle. The fact that we live to find meaning and purpose in life is not meant to destroy or replace the law of effect or the pleasure principle.

REFLECTIONS

We invite you to use this space to record your reflections, feelings, and insights. May this experience deepen your self-understanding and connection with others.

_____
_____
_____
_____
_____
_____
_____
_____
_____
_____
_____
_____
_____
_____
_____
_____
_____
_____
_____
_____
_____
_____
_____
_____
_____
_____
_____
_____

Personal Change Occurs Gradually In Steps
and/or
Can Change In A Short Time

Personal change is usually slow

When driven by the environment.

Personal change will faster go

When perceptions provide enlightenment.

Personal change comes gradually.

But with a change of heart

It comes so suddenly.

The majority of experimental research findings in psychology would lead to the conclusion that our change or growth is slow and gradual. There are exceptions as the adolescent growth spurt or the "ahh ha" experience in solving a problem. But on the main, observations and experiments show a gradual improvement as a result of rewarded practice. From B.F. Skinner's theories and confirmed research supporting behavior modification, the recommended procedure for changing another's behavior is to gradually reward successive approximations of the desired behavior.

In contrast, if and when a person's perception or perspective changes and this can happen suddenly, the behavior changes suddenly. The phenomenological concept is: "perceptions at the moment of action are the cause of behavior." Thus, how one perceives is the critical and most important element in human change. Changes in spirit can occur quickly, dramatically, and completely. The behavior then will markedly change to be congruent with the change in the perception or inner spirit.

REFLECTIONS

We invite you to use this space to record your reflections, feelings, and insights. May this experience deepen your self-understanding and connection with others.

_____
_____
_____
_____
_____
_____
_____
_____
_____
_____
_____
_____
_____
_____
_____
_____
_____
_____
_____
_____
_____
_____
_____
_____
_____
_____
_____
_____

Understanding Self and Others Is A Science
and/or
Understanding Self Is An Art

The laws of behavior come from science.

But understanding another is an art.

It comes from seeing another's heart.

Thus, the heart is the place to start.

The disciplines for understanding humans have come to define themselves as a science. This is understandable because science has been so successful in explaining the natural world. If you want to understand yourself and others in a scientific way you would either conduct experiments or draw information from those who have conducted experiments on human beings. From these experiments, you would create the laws that govern behavior and then you would apply these laws in a systematic way to yourself and others whom you have analyzed.

On the other hand, the understanding of self and others might be better conceived as an art. If each individual is a unique spirit, the spirit must be considered for an adequate understanding. Science does not and cannot offer all the requisite information. Knowing this, and also knowing that we must come to some understanding of self and others we would then be wise to borrow information from other sources. In fact, borrows from many other sources. Subjective judgments must be made, the situation must be considered, and you need to see who this person is, what they are feeling, and respond to the spirit as well as to cognitions and the body. So, would understanding humans be more accurately categorized as art rather than science?

REFLECTIONS

We invite you to use this space to record your reflections, feelings, and insights. May this experience deepen your self-understanding and connection with others.

_____
_____
_____
_____
_____
_____
_____
_____
_____
_____
_____
_____
_____
_____
_____
_____
_____
_____
_____
_____
_____
_____
_____
_____
_____
_____
_____
_____
_____

Understanding Self Requires Analysis
and/or
Understanding Self Requires Synthesis

A man is more

than the sum of his parts.

Instead, he's a moving complexity

And must be understood artistically.

There is a better way to understand another.

It's not analysis but synthesis.

With synthesis, you create more completeness

And see more wholeness.

The word analysis is almost synonymous with trying to understand by considering causal factors. Because of popular psychoanalysis, we use the word freely to include figuring out the most basic elements that drive the human being, and what produces these elements of personality and action. Understanding causation is the goal. We do this by analyzing and by analyzing we mean to classify the person into subunits and parts until we know how to better treat the person.

In contrast to this, understanding may be harmed more than helped by analysis. The needed skill is to envision or perceive the whole person and to see things that may not be apparent. Understanding may require creating a more complete holistic picture of the other person. People who do this will see and find a more complete description of life, purpose, and meaning.

REFLECTIONS

We invite you to use this space to record your reflections, feelings, and insights. May this experience deepen your self-understanding and connection with others.

_____
_____
_____
_____
_____
_____
_____
_____
_____
_____
_____
_____
_____
_____
_____
_____
_____
_____
_____
_____
_____
_____
_____
_____
_____
_____
_____
_____
_____

SECTION VI: *"CHOICES ABOUT UNDERSTANDING OTHERS"*

Focus on casual background	*and/or* Focus on the present and spirit
Trust in intellect and reasoning	*and/or* Trust feelings/conscience
Believe truth is relative/unknowable	*and/or* Believe absolutes can be known
Utilize only the best method for knowing	*and/or* Utilize all ways of knowing
Use laws for understanding	*and/or* Use insights for understanding

While the word spirit has been part of our conversation, it might be well to mention a similarity between conceptions of the 'self' and 'spirit'. The early view of self is best seen as a derivative of Descartes's notion of an autonomous entity directing the body. This view is called the punctuated self by Charles Taylor, who compares this notion with a 'romantic self' that comes endowed with positive, growth-promoting tendencies that had roots in the thinking of the Enlightenment. The 'existential self 'of Sartre and others was a choosing, self-selecting entity that had to choose to be and in so doing constituted itself or created the future self. This has been referred to as the 'self-constituted self' Later Hermeneutic ideas would see the person more as a happening or moving event rather than an entity. In this situation, the self would have a forward movement but the extent to which it comes endowed or is self-constructed or constituted is open, but the general tone is still self-creating. Emmanual Levinas, a French moral philosopher, believes an "I" exists always in the present but the 'I' always exists with an ethical responsibility to the "other". "The psyche in the soul is the other in me."

Focus On Causal Background
and/or
Focus On The Present And Spirit

We are not the product of our past conditioning.

It is present perceptions that determine daily living.

We can reinterpret what's in our memory.

To reshape and escape the past to live free.

You might say that the past no longer exists, it is gone. It cannot touch the present for if it did it would be in the present. To overcome this logical impossibility theorists, say perceptions at the moment of action determine behavior. Of course, past experiences do influence present perceptions, but the word is influence not cause. The past influences present behavior by changing perceptions. Present perceptions or cognitions at the moment of action are of course caused by a wider number of things such as thought, the situation, the presence or absence of loved ones, and so forth. While the past may influence our present perceptions, the past does not entirely cause present perceptions and thus doesn't entirely cause behavior.

A more accurate and meaningful way to understand a person is to study how they perceive the world. While it is impossible to change the past it is possible to change perceptions of the past. We can view this realization as complimentary or compatible with free agency. But even more important than perception is the spirit within. It is much more direct and important to discern, feel, and reach another person's present spirit than to intellectually analyze their past.

REFLECTIONS

We invite you to use this space to record your reflections, feelings, and insights. May this experience deepen your self-understanding and connection with others.

_____

_____

_____

_____

_____

_____

_____

_____

_____

_____

_____

_____

_____

_____

_____

_____

_____

_____

_____

_____

_____

_____

_____

_____

_____

_____

_____

Trust In Intellect And Reasoning
and/or
Trust Feelings/Conscience

We sometimes discover an insight;

One which comes from feeling not reasoning.

Feelings can help us solve a problem

So misleading thinking can be forgotten.

We all need insights to understand other people. And of course, reasoning is the traditional and time-honored method to arrive at insights. However, if one examines the histories of great discoveries in science and other intellectual endeavors, we find that the greatest discoveries often come in unexpected moments and in ways that were not predicted. Researchers have tried to find the rules that govern creative discovery and usually find that some kind of sudden, subconscious, unexpected, novel, new, visual, or auditory experience is what delivers the insight.

Because most of our dealings with people often have a moral component, the insights can come from our moral sensitivity or what we have been calling conscience. The best way to understand and treat another is frequently revealed by our conscience rather than in addition to a rational intellectual or scientific analysis.

REFLECTIONS

We invite you to use this space to record your reflections, feelings, and insights. May this experience deepen your self-understanding and connection with others.

_____
_____
_____
_____
_____
_____
_____
_____
_____
_____
_____
_____
_____
_____
_____
_____
_____
_____
_____
_____
_____
_____
_____
_____
_____
_____
_____
_____

Believe Truth Is Relative/Unknowable
and/or
Believe Absolutes Can Be Known

We are sometimes confused by moral rules,

Especially when we can't make an absolute prediction.

Still, an absolute truth can appear in a decision

For a unique individual in a unique situation.

If there is nothing other than matter and energy, then all truths are simply descriptions of fact. And then when it comes to moral statements or statements of ought, there can be no certainty about what to do.

On the other hand, if a spirit exists, if conscience exists, and if a supreme being exists then to understand self and others there are other ways to find and know right and wrong, good and bad. These may or may not follow from laws and abstractions that are absolute throughout the universe but are known for the unique individual in a specific context or situation. Thus, we don't have to depend exclusively on having abstract moral absolutes to obtain certainty of right or wrong. Instead, one can find right or wrong by methods such as intuition, moral sensitivity, and revelation. It is possible to know what is right or wrong, good or bad, in an absolute way; but it is known in the concrete situation.

REFLECTIONS

We invite you to use this space to record your reflections, feelings, and insights. May this experience deepen your self-understanding and connection with others.

_____
_____
_____
_____
_____
_____
_____
_____
_____
_____
_____
_____
_____
_____
_____
_____
_____
_____
_____
_____
_____
_____
_____
_____
_____
_____
_____
_____
_____

Utilize Only Best Method For Knowing
and/or
Utilize All Ways Of Knowing

When using only one way of knowing,

A person's ignorance is showing.

Most of us have known a person who we can describe as "a matter of fac guy" or "an objective person." Such persons bring to the situation an analysis or a heightened ability to analyze a situation. These persons bring to bear the appropriate laws and principles that regulate such a situation, and they reason out the logical implications and know what to do. This is a method that fits almost all situations. And the method is logical positivism or science. There is definitely a respect for people like this. They are needed, and they are very successful when they are objective and analytical.

While we might be successful in life by objective, analytical, and scientific approaches the general observation is that such persons are often lacking in some very important ways in some situations. The most obvious deficiency is in the area of human relationships where such a person overlooks intangible feelings and sensitivities that are difficult to discern.

Although they may choose to be scientific these individuals can improve or benefit if they also employ knowledge and truth from other sources. Earlier we mentioned that traditional culture yields many truths as does literature, traditions, and theologies. Perhaps more important in understanding another person is what we have referred to as experiential living. We learn about another person by walking in their shoes, sharing their lives, and attentively listening and observing.

REFLECTIONS

We invite you to use this space to record your reflections, feelings, and insights. May this experience deepen your self-understanding and connection with others.

_____
_____
_____
_____
_____
_____
_____
_____
_____
_____
_____
_____
_____
_____
_____
_____
_____
_____
_____
_____
_____
_____
_____
_____
_____
_____
_____

Use Laws For Understanding
and/or
Use Insights For Understanding

It is impossible to memorize

A moral law for each situation.

But moral insights help each decision

And do so for every occasion.

When we are analytical, factual, and rational in analyzing a problem we usually have in mind a goal to find a principle or a law that regulates whatever we are observing. In the case of people, we try to find a principle that is at work here. While psychologists have done this for almost a century, it is safe to say that there are not many laws of behavior accepted or that have unanimous agreement, or even come close to the consensual agreement similar to those found in the natural and physical sciences. This must tell us something about using this method to find laws that govern human behavior.

But even more important is the observation that when controversial principles or laws are applied, they do not work because of the unique circumstances that surround each person. Abstractions often do not work because of individual differences between people. Thus, it may be more productive to seek and find, as a guide for understanding others, the insights that come in the given situation at the moment. These could be called insights coming from an external spiritual source, coming from the spirit within, or coming from your own experience as it becomes attuned to the spirit of the other person and to the situation that exists. They also could be known in other ways that would not be called spiritual but are still insightful.

REFLECTIONS

We invite you to use this space to record your reflections, feelings, and insights. May this experience deepen your self-understanding and connection with others.

_____
_____
_____
_____
_____
_____
_____
_____
_____
_____
_____
_____
_____
_____
_____
_____
_____
_____
_____
_____
_____
_____
_____
_____
_____
_____
_____

SECTION VII: *"CHOICES ABOUT YOUR RELATIONSHIP WITH OTHERS"*

Change others   *and/or* Accept others as they are

Focus on tolerance   *and/or* Focus on love

Seek service   *and/or* Give service

Use high power when   *and/or* Use low power when
relating   relating

Retain past   *and/or* Forgive

Label and categorize others   *and/or* Be non-judgmental

Use others to achieve   *and/or* Help others succeed
success

Expect only correct   *and/or* Respect other's perspective
perspective

Educate for behavior change   *and/or* Educate the heart and spirit

Teach correct perspective   *and/or* Build upon the perspective
                                  of others

Withdraw when non-   *and/or* Care for others
rewarding

Change Others
and/or
Accept Others As They Are

Change another?

Most often it's better

To do the reverse

And change yourself first.

Assume that it is good to help others. However, does that mean changing and shaping others for the better? There are several professions including teachers, therapists, and social workers whose commendable job is interpreted as changing others for the better. However, maybe the best way to help others is not to begin with an agenda of changing them.

Perhaps the most beneficial growth and development in another person results from acceptance rather than beginning with the intention to change them. This may be so even in a situation where no change is required such as establishing and developing a healthy relationship with another person. The problems that emerge from setting out to intentionally change the other person can be circumvented.

In relationships the first helping, healthy response is accepting and loving the other rather than changing. In a concrete situation like marriage, rather than trying to change your partner so they become more lovable change yourself so you are more loving.

REFLECTIONS

We invite you to use this space to record your reflections, feelings, and insights. May this experience deepen your self-understanding and connection with others.

_____

_____

_____

_____

_____

_____

_____

_____

_____

_____

_____

_____

_____

_____

_____

_____

_____

_____

_____

_____

_____

_____

_____

_____

_____

_____

_____

Focus On Tolerance
and/or
Focus On Love

Tolerance is valuable.

Love is wonderful.

Love makes things delightful

And tolerance will follow.

The virtue of tolerance receives a great deal of approval in popular modern culture today. The need to eliminate prejudices of all kinds has resulted in the systematic education of the general population to be tolerant of others. Thus, tolerance is one of our most popular virtues. We are asked to tolerate those who are different, and whose lifestyles conflict with ours, and we should also tolerate those we dislike. This tolerance virtue is of course good, but is there not a higher and better way?

Love is more than tolerance, even more than acceptance. Love involves acting and doing something for the benefit of another. Love also includes positive regard, sharing, caring, affection, and giving. When one looks broadly at the concept of love, we see that it is much greater than tolerance. Therefore, in our relationships, it is more important to strive towards the love of the other. Love is the greater virtue.

Technically speaking love and tolerance are not opposites. Nevertheless, in everyday life, they are a choice. As pointed out earlier the choices between opposites may often fall in between. Sometimes they vacillate from situation to situation and time to time and place to place. The importance of this is found in the benefit and positive development that comes from making choices.

REFLECTIONS

We invite you to use this space to record your reflections, feelings, and insights. May this experience deepen your self-understanding and connection with others.

_____

_____

_____

_____

_____

_____

_____

_____

_____

_____

_____

_____

_____

_____

_____

_____

_____

_____

_____

_____

_____

_____

_____

_____

_____

_____

_____

_____

Seek Service
and/or
Give Service

Receiving is most often sought

And done without any thought.

Giving is more rewarding

And always more fulfilling.

Many well-intentioned books focus on Influence. I published one myself. The way our society is organized requires the service of others in maintaining our automobiles, typing our reports, and fixing our appliances. We tend to seek service from others using influence. We tend to think the successful person is the one who is able to have others do as much as possible in the way of service for oneself.

Service, however, is a way to become a better person through the performance of the service. Therefore, service given rather than received is to be sought. Giving service is more important than finding ways to have others serve us through obligation, payment, friendship, or influence. Again, both receiving and giving service will inevitably take place yet placing one over the other is an important determining choice for you.

REFLECTIONS

We invite you to use this space to record your reflections, feelings, and insights. May this experience deepen your self-understanding and connection with others.

_____
_____
_____
_____
_____
_____
_____
_____
_____
_____
_____
_____
_____
_____
_____
_____
_____
_____
_____
_____
_____
_____
_____
_____
_____

Use High Power When Relating
and/or
Use Low Power When Relating

So natural, so common, so tempting

To use force and power when relating.

But, with being gentle, accepting, and loving.

Influencing will be more enduring.

We sometimes describe a person in positive terms as being powerful. These are people who have at their disposal strength, wealth, influence, and other ways to either subtly or forcefully cause others to do their will. In relationships, we also see this as a person who dominates the relationship and can use their many powers, including subtle ones of verbal persuasion, and emotion to influence others. This person is often considered the most admirable.

At one time I published a parenting textbook in which I analyzed all the parenting techniques and outcomes associated with power. A general conclusion emerged. It was that the use of low power by parents was associated with more positive outcomes in children. The reason for this may not be entirely clear, but part of it refers to the better relationships that emerge when the relationship is not based on one or more parties using high power to influence. Rather, low-power methods such as sharing feelings, mutual problem solving, developing consideration for the wellbeing of the other person, and empathy were proven to be more successful.

REFLECTIONS

We invite you to use this space to record your reflections, feelings, and insights. May this experience deepen your self-understanding and connection with others.

_____
_____
_____
_____
_____
_____
_____
_____
_____
_____
_____
_____
_____
_____
_____
_____
_____
_____
_____
_____
_____
_____
_____
_____
_____
_____
_____
_____
_____

Retain Past
and/or
Forgive

Having a long memory

May just prolong misery.

Better to forgive easily

And live life more freely.

The virtue of having a long memory does not always benefit a person in human relationships. Of course, we want to intelligently be aware of past tendencies of the other person so that negative experiences can be avoided or prevented. But if people are to change for the better, they need to be believed and accepted in their changed form. Retaining the past is a definite detriment to this.

Recently, several excellent books have been written on the benefits of forgiveness. It seems very clear from the studies that enduring relationships emerge when there is more forgiving. Change is much more possible when low, not high-power methods are employed. Love with trust blossoms when forgiveness rather than retaining past grievances is the way to be.

REFLECTIONS

We invite you to use this space to record your reflections, feelings, and insights. May this experience deepen your self-understanding and connection with others.

_____
_____
_____
_____
_____
_____
_____
_____
_____
_____
_____
_____
_____
_____
_____
_____
_____
_____
_____
_____
_____
_____
_____
_____
_____
_____
_____
_____
_____

Label And Categorize Others
and/or
Be Non-Judgmental

We need; we like to understand others.

So, we label to make things predictable.

But when using a broad label

We fail to see the individual.

In our relationships, we want to know who we are relating with, or what kind of person we have in front of us. It is very natural when using an analytic technique to erect categories, even categories of people. We then place those who are in front of us into these constructed categories. The expected benefit is increased predictability of the other person because now we know what kind of person they are.

There are serious disadvantages to the categorization procedure. Once categorized the other person has a hard time changing because they tend to believe the category as well. But even if they disbelieve the categorization and do change, others find it difficult to accept the change and thus a relationship does not evolve and is stuck where it is. The way to avoid the problems of categorization is to be non-judgmental in the first place. If one accepts the fact that people are constantly changing, then categories become much less useful because people are constantly moving in and out of all of the categories that are constructed. But it is not just the accuracy of the judgment that is problematic. It is the judgment itself. The judgment usually is a criticism and in relationships judgment and criticism lead to defensiveness, withdrawal, hurt feelings, and of course, these are detrimental to the relationship.

REFLECTIONS

We invite you to use this space to record your reflections, feelings, and insights. May this experience deepen your self-understanding and connection with others.

_____
_____
_____
_____
_____
_____
_____
_____
_____
_____
_____
_____
_____
_____
_____
_____
_____
_____
_____
_____
_____
_____
_____
_____
_____
_____
_____
_____

Use Others To Achieve Success
and/or
Help Others Succeed

When you meet someone new

What do you see and do?

Are they there to benefit you

Or do you want to help them too?

Years ago, a psycho-therapist, Eric Fromm, described two opposite personalities. A manipulative personality vs. a productive personality. He pointed out that in our society the manipulative personality uses others to accomplish his own ends. For the manipulative person, other people are seen as a means to an end; the end being one's own rewards.

The productive personality is a person who tries to produce benefits for all concerned; the self as well as others. In essence, the productive person is one who moves ahead by helping others as well as helping oneself. So, in the life of a productive person helping others facilitates helping oneself, and visa-versa.

If one can truly see the spirit of another person, then it is much easier to understand and help them in the relationship. This is done by not viewing and using the other person for one's own ends. If you see the person primarily as an object, not as a spirit, then it is easier to fall into the mode of using the other person for self-benefit.

REFLECTIONS

We invite you to use this space to record your reflections, feelings, and insights. May this experience deepen your self-understanding and connection with others.

_____
_____
_____
_____
_____
_____
_____
_____
_____
_____
_____
_____
_____
_____
_____
_____
_____
_____
_____
_____
_____
_____
_____
_____
_____
_____
_____
_____
_____
_____
_____

Educate For Behavior Change
and/or
Educate the Heart And Spirit

Changing behavior is superficial.

There is something more desirable.

There is a better place to start.

It is to change their heart.

The word educate is used because it refers to a broad range of activities used to enhance the knowledge, actions, and feelings of another person. It includes more than just teaching. Educate is a highly commendable term, and almost all people must be educated in the course of their lives. Parents educate their children for life, as do teachers, service workers, *friends, pastors, and any admirable public servant.*

But the goal is important. If we seek only behavioral change much will be lacking. All of us have seen a relationship in which the parties argue to the point that each agrees begrudgingly to change their actions or behavior only to satisfy the other person's wishes. This will prove to be an inadequate outcome from a relationship point of view.

A much higher way to change is to educate the heart or spirit of another person. This usually cannot be done by telling or teaching but can be brought about by providing experiences, setting an example, and honestly sharing one's confidences and inner feelings in the hopes that the other person's heart will be changed. When a person's spirit or heart is changed behavior will follow. It becomes a change that can be trusted.

REFLECTIONS

We invite you to use this space to record your reflections, feelings, and insights. May this experience deepen your self-understanding and connection with others.

_____
_____
_____
_____
_____
_____
_____
_____
_____
_____
_____
_____
_____
_____
_____
_____
_____
_____
_____
_____
_____
_____
_____
_____
_____
_____
_____
_____
_____

Expect Only Correct Perspective
and/or
Respect Other's Perspectives

Please, just see things my way.

Because I can't see things your way.

However, I will listen to what you have to say

And hope we can agree in at least some small way.

In relationships, we often notice that each person has their own point of view and when these are different the relationship often suffers, and when they become more similar the relationship seems to run smoothly. If in case of conflicting perspectives one approach is to get the other person to view things the way we do. This is beneficial to the relationship but is usually done at great costs and difficulty. Typically, the person resists, counters, argues, and tries to maintain their own position.

However, if we start by trying to build agreements upon the perspective and spirit of the other person more progress will take place in the growth of the relationship and the outcome and solution will be more stable. There are many reasons for this outcome so it is important to first try to see, comprehend, and understand the perspective of the other. This perspective best comes from seeing the spirit of the other person. If we come to see and understand their spirit, we are more likely to see their perspective. When we know their perspective, we are in a key place to intelligently do our part in making the relationship better.

REFLECTIONS

We invite you to use this space to record your reflections, feelings, and insights. May this experience deepen your self-understanding and connection with others.

_____
_____
_____
_____
_____
_____
_____
_____
_____
_____
_____
_____
_____
_____
_____
_____
_____
_____
_____
_____
_____
_____
_____
_____
_____
_____
_____
_____

Withdraw When Non-Rewarding
and/or
Care for Others Indefinitely

When things don't go your way

You could just walk away.

Instead, it's best to stay.

And work to make a better day.

Sometimes a person fails you.

And you wonder what to say or do.

Become the person who so lives.

To receive the peace that forgiveness gives.

Generally, in relationships, we do our best to develop a good relationship. Our individual efforts vary greatly depending upon our desire for the relationship to continue, and our own perseverance. But, at some point, when things don't go our way, we decide that it is better to get out of the relationship. Everyone has received this good advice sometime in their life. The opposite response to getting out of a relationship that isn't going our way is to increase our love and acceptance of the other. It is well expressed in the Christian philosophies of how many times you should forgive. Part of our personal development lies in our ability to stay in relationships in a caring way for longer periods of time, even indefinitely. Still, sometimes it's best to withdraw.

REFLECTIONS

We invite you to use this space to record your reflections, feelings, and insights. May this experience deepen your self-understanding and connection with others.

_____
_____
_____
_____
_____
_____
_____
_____
_____
_____
_____
_____
_____
_____
_____
_____
_____
_____
_____
_____
_____
_____
_____
_____
_____
_____
_____

Growing Slowly
and/or
Progressing Faster With Choices

Choices determine how fast or slow we grow.

Choices expand what we come to know.

They are a blessing,

Without them we would

Stop progressing.

Perhaps it would be helpful to summarize what has happened in this second section of the book. Presented are choices you can make about your being, then choices that you can make about understanding others, and finally choices you can make about your relationship with others. You may have noticed that the choices are about more and more specific things and are more difficult and less clear-cut.

Choices about your being are somewhat abstract, as are choices about others. But choices about your relationships become very specific and focused on what you do. Perhaps this is the whole point of the book. The questions and choices are what influence relationships with others. We also have a relationship with God that is not discussed here. However, almost all the choices you made about a relationship with others would apply to your relationship with God.

If you have been able to answer questions about yourself, about truth and knowledge, and your identity then it is my hope that these questions and choices provide a basis and foundation upon which to live longer as a free agent.

REFLECTIONS

We invite you to use this space to record your reflections, feelings, and insights. May this experience deepen your self-understanding and connection with others.

_____
_____
_____
_____
_____
_____
_____
_____
_____
_____
_____
_____
_____
_____
_____
_____
_____
_____
_____
_____
_____
_____
_____
_____
_____
_____
_____
_____

ABOUT PROFESSOR LARRY CYRIL JENSEN

Professor Jensen was born in 1938 and grew up in Wyoming, Montana, and Colorado. He is married to Janet and is a father to 10 children, 33 grandchildren, and 3 great-grandchildren.

After graduating from Wheat Ridge High School in Colorado he received B.S. and M.S. Degrees from Brigham Young University and his Ph.D. degree from Michigan State University.

Professor Jensen has taught at the following universities:

1. Michigan State University
2. State University of New York at Potsdam
3. Brigham Young University at Provo
4. Brigham Young University at Hawaii
5. Utah State University
6. Southern Virginia University

He has consulted for:

1. Research for Better Schools
2. Journal of Child Development
3. Psychological Reports and Perceptual Motor Skills
4. Family Research Center Brigham Young University
5. Provo and Salt Lake City Public Schools
6. Institute for Population Studies in Exeter England

His books include the following:

1. What's Right What's Wrong
2. Understanding and Using Social Influence Techniques
3. That's Not Fair
4. Moral Reasoning: A Philosophical and Psychological Integration
5. Responsibility and Morality
6. Feelings: Helping Children Understand Emotions
7. History of Moral Education
8. Stepping Into Step-Parenting
9. Adolescence
10. Parenting: An Applied Textbook
11. Family Feminism
12. Families: The Key to a Prosperous and Compassionate Society in the 21st Century

He has published multiple scholarly articles in the following journals:

1. Psychological Reports
2. Utah Personnel and Guidance Association Research Bulletin
3. Proceedings of the American Educational Research Association
4. Journal of Educational Psychology
5. Developmental Psychology
6. Journal of Experimental Psychology
7. Journal of Genetic Psychology
8. British Journal of Social and Clinical Psychology
9. Journal of Moral Education
10. Education
11. Educational and Psychological Measurement
12. Psychology in the Schools
13. Sex Roles
14. Journal of Psychology
15. Adolescence
16. International Journal of Social Psychiatry
17. Youth and Society
18. Journal for the Scientific Study or Religion
19. Journal of Business Ethics
20. Family Perspectives
21. Journal of Personality Assessment
22. American Educational Research Journal
23. Addictive Behaviors
24. Journal of Cross-Cultural Psychology
25. Journal of Research and Development in Education
26. Family Therapy
27. Religion and Public Education
28. The Family in America
29. Youth and Adolescence

ABOUT BRIDGER LEE JENSEN

Bridger Lee Jensen is a thought leader in contemporary mental wellness, religious philosophy, and personal development. With a distinguished career spanning over two decades in mental health, he is dedicated to fostering emotional well-being, self-discovery, and holistic healing.

Jensen's intellectual foundation was shaped by his parents, particularly his father, Dr. Larry Cyril Jensen—a psychologist, philosopher, and theologian. From an early age, Bridger engaged in deep discussions on existence, consciousness, and the psychological frameworks that shape belief systems. His upbringing immersed him in psychology, philosophy, and religion, fostering a lifelong passion for understanding the human mind and spirit. His mother also played a vital role, demonstrating the power of love, perseverance, and the importance of family through her actions.

These formative influences led Jensen to establish Singularism, a contemporary philosophy that harmonizes existential thought, cognitive psychology, and spiritual practice. Singularism is dedicated to personal growth, emotional healing, and the pursuit of meaning in life.

Beyond Singularism, Jensen founded Mental Gurus, an AI-driven mental health platform addressing the global need for accessible psychological care. His work integrates timeless wisdom with innovative technology, providing scalable solutions for self-exploration, emotional resilience, and clarity of purpose.

Before founding Singularism, Jensen spent years in mental health counseling, family therapy, and adventure-based therapeutic programs. His expertise in transformative therapy is recognized across disciplines, from academic research to direct clinical applications. His contributions to wellness programs have influenced the development of new approaches to mental health and personal growth.

At the core of Jensen's work is his devotion to family. A father of four, he holds family as his highest value, seeing it as the foundation for personal and spiritual growth. His belief in healing and enlightenment begins at home, shaping how he approaches mental health, philosophy, and personal development.

As a thought leader, Jensen embodies existential humility in his pursuit of truth, self-discovery, and the advancement of human consciousness. His writings, teachings, and innovations continue to shape modern approaches to spirituality, mental wellness, and self-improvement.

For more about Bridger's work, visit:

- Singularism
- Psychedelictherapyjourney.com
- LinkedIn
- Bridgerleejensen.com

www.ingramcontent.com/pod-product-compliance
Lightning Source LLC
Chambersburg PA
CBHW030309130626
46549CB00002B/774